A
BOOK
IS A PRESENT
YOU CAN OPEN
AGAIN
AND
AGAIN

This Book Belongs To

Fred Mestman Elias

© Mary Engelbreit

At the Zoo

by Douglas Florian

Greenwillow Books, New York

A sepia pen line and colored pencils
were used for the full-color art.
The text type is ITC Cheltenham Light.

a division of William Morrow & Company, Inc.,
1350 Avenue of the Americas, New York, NY 10019
Printed in Hong Kong by South China
Printing Company (1988) Ltd.
First Edition   10 9 8 7 6 5 4 3 2 1

Library of Congress Cataloging-in-Publication Data

Florian, Douglas.
At the zoo / Douglas Florian.
p.   cm.
Summary: Labeled drawings portray animals at the zoo.
ISBN 0-688-09628-X.   ISBN 0-688-09629-8 (lib. bdg.)
1. Zoo animals—Pictorial works—Juvenile literature.
[1. Zoo animals—Pictorial works.]   I. Title.
QL77.5.F56   1992
590'.74'4—dc20   89-77727   CIP   AC

For Marie, Naomi,
Ariel, and Sammy,
and a day at the zoo

At the zoo

Kangaroo

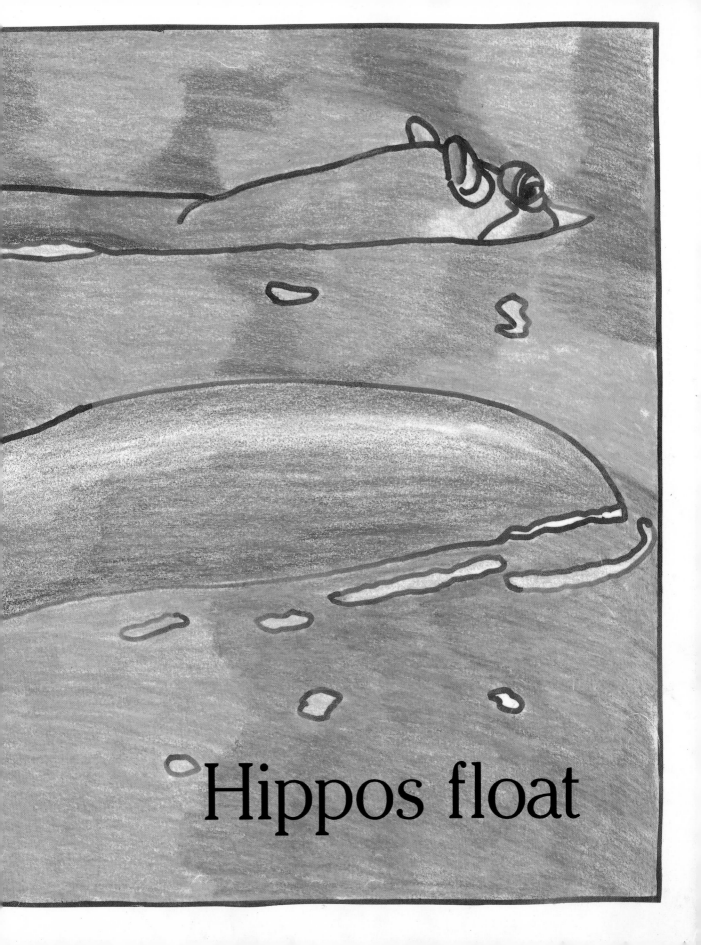

Hippos float

Mountain goat

Zoo guide

Camel ride

Polar bears

Baby hares

Tall giraffe

Moose and calf

Monkeys swing

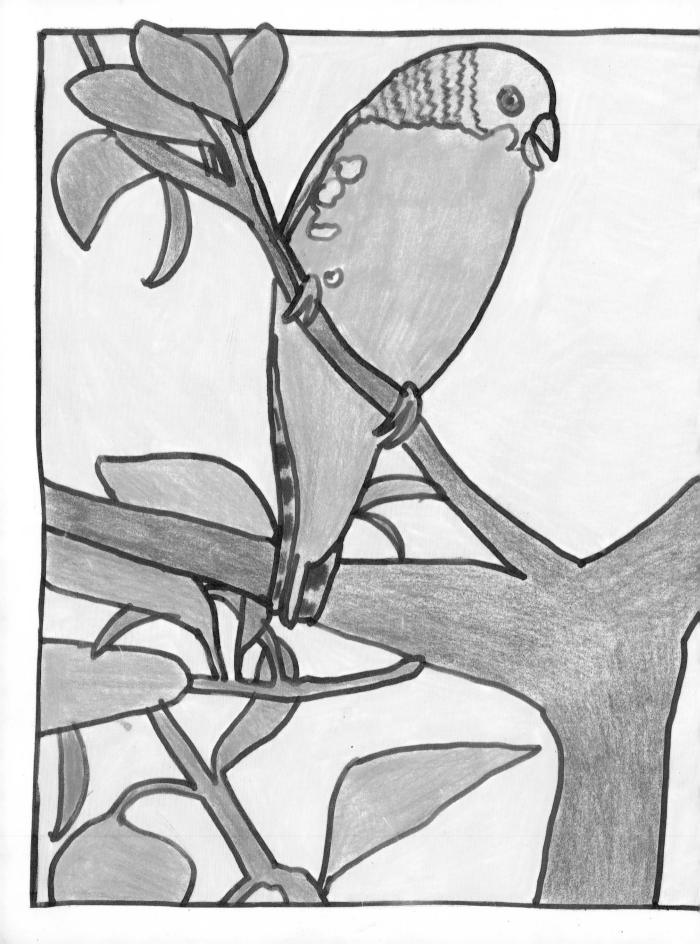

Songbirds sing

Koalas climb

Closing time